Cardinals

Blondyz Snapshotz

Annette Wiseman

Copyright © 2012 Author Name

All rights reserved.

ISBN: 1544721757
ISBN-13: 9781544721750

DEDICATION

To those we love, and the memories that keep us going.

Focus on the good stuff!

AW

Love

Never

Fails

I am first an animal lover.
Then a photographer who enjoys taking snapshotz of life.
Somewhere in there, I am an artist.
This is me, this is who I am.

I am always with you.

Even in the most quarrelsome surroundings, the grateful heart finds peace.

It's a beautiful day!

AW

Listen with your heart, not your mind.

Annette Wiseman

Birds sing after a storm;

why shouldn't people feel as free

To delight in whatever remains to them?

-Rose F Kennedy

Never forget yesterday, but always live for today...

Because you never know what tomorrow can bring, or what it can take away.

LIFE

...is
the greatest journey
you will ever be on.

visitors

Choose Peace.

Nature always wears the colors of the spirit.

-Ralph Waldo Emerson

Even so, it is well with my soul.

31

There are two ways to get enough.

One is to continue to accumulate more and more.

The other is to desire less.

So much of what you are is where you've been.

Even a snow storm, can be beautiful.

Enjoy the little things in life...

IT'S NOT ALWAYS ABOUT THE PERFECT PICTURE,
BUT MORE SO … THE PERFECT MOMENT.

It is easy to love the beautiful critters that come to the yard.
I make sure they have plenty of food and water.
Word gets around, they tell their friends, and they tell their friends – and pretty soon it's a party in the backyard.
I'm always watching for "someone" new.

www.ingramcontent.com/pod-product-compliance
Lightning Source LLC
Chambersburg PA
CBHW060836290526
45792CB00006BB/1947